# THE WORLD'S
# CRAZIEST
## DRINKING GAMES

D1332840

summersdale

THE WORLD'S CRAZIEST DRINKING GAMES

Text by Agatha Russell

Image credits:
shot glass © Agnieszka Karpinska/Shutterstock.com, dice © Martial Red/Shutterstock.com,
beer bottles © Yoko Design/Shutterstock.com, cup © Sudowoodo/Shutterstock.com

An Hachette UK Company
www.hachette.co.uk

Summersdale Publishers Ltd
Part of Octopus Publishing Group Limited
Carmelite House
50 Victoria Embankment
LONDON
EC4Y 0DZ
UK

www.summersdale.com

Printed and bound in China

ISBN: 978-1-80007-434-7

Substantial discounts on bulk quantities of Summersdale books are available to corporations,
professional associations and other organizations. For details contact general enquiries:
telephone: +44 (0) 1243 771107 or email: enquiries@summersdale.com.

Disclaimer: The publisher urges care and caution in the pursuit of any of the activities
represented in this book. This book is intended for use by adults only. Please drink responsibly.

# CONTENTS

# INTRODUCTION

No matter where we are in the world, the heady combination of our favourite tipple and a great game succeeds in making nights to remember... or not, as is often the case. This truly bizarre collection is divided into countries, accompanied by a list of what is needed to play – needless to say, each game requires alcohol. So flick through, find your favourite games, and make your pre-drinks, your party or your night out the world's craziest.

# DRINKING RULES FOR THIS BOOK

Whenever this book instructs you to "take a drink", you are expected to do so but with a degree of modesty – for example, by using the two-finger rule. Hold two fingers horizontally across the glass and use that as a measure for the instruction. This also applies for drinking penalties.

If you want to make things even more interesting, you'll find some fun restrictions suggested by partygoers from around the globe on the next page. These are sure to spice up the games throughout the evening. If any of the following rules are broken, you must take a drink.

# DRINKING RULES FROM AROUND THE GLOBE

Canada: No swearing.

England: You must drink with your little finger pointed out.

Australia: No first names. For example, you could refer to people as you see them – be as creative as you like: lobster legs, crab hands and so on.

China: Don't raise your glass higher than your host's or your elders', as it is considered to be disrespectful.

Russia: You must make a toast before every round of drinks.

Germany: When saying cheers, you must clink glasses and maintain eye contact, for it is said that if you do not you will suffer nine years of bad sex! You must say prost ("cheers") if you are drinking beer, and for everything else, say zum wohl ("to your health").

France: When topping up, serve women first.

Japan: Never pour your own drink.

Iceland: Everyone must drink with their left hand. (If anyone is spotted using their right hand, the person who spotted them must chant, "BUFFALO, BUFFALO, BUFFALO". Everyone joins in while banging on the table, until the culprit has downed their drink.)

# I KNEW I WAS DRUNK: I FELT SOPHISTICATED AND COULDN'T PRONOUNCE IT.

**Anonymous**

# AMERICA
# THE MOST
# LIKELY TO

### Difficulty:

### What you will need:

Three or more players

# You'd better hope your friends think well of you!

Players sit in a circle. Going round the circle one at a time, each player asks a "most likely" question. For example: who is most likely to be mistaken for the Queen? Or, who is most likely to be arrested for bad behaviour?

On the count of three, everyone points to the person they think best fits the bill. Players take a drink for every person pointing at them. The game continues in this way. Simple but fun!

# AMERICA
# STRAIGHT
# FACE

## Difficulty:

## What you will need:

Four or more players
A bowl
A pen
Paper

# Whatever you do, do not laugh!

Tear the paper up into small strips for each player. Your task is to each write down the weirdest, funniest, most random statement. Your aim is to make your opponents crack up with uncontrollable laughter. Put everyone's strips of comedy gold into a bowl in the middle of the table. Jumble them up. Now the game may begin. One by one, players take it in turns to pick a piece of paper from the bowl. With your straightest face possible, read the sentence. Any players found to be smirking, concealing giggles or outright cackling will have to drink!

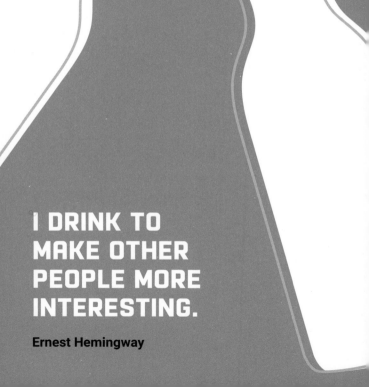

**I DRINK TO MAKE OTHER PEOPLE MORE INTERESTING.**

**Ernest Hemingway**

# AMERICA
# SLIP IT IN

### Difficulty:

### What you will need:
Five or more players

## Drunk and inconspicuous...

This is a perfect idea for a house party, but it can be done anywhere – you just need a big group of people to blend in to! As the host, you need to come up with a "slip it in" phrase for each of your guests. These can be as crazy or as strange as you like. For example, a good one could be "you look like a pilot" or "I hate popcorn". It is up to your guests to fit these phrases into conversation without being found out.

If the phrase is spoken and no one guesses in five minutes then everyone in the room has to drink, though if someone is discovered saying their phrase, then that person must drink.

# DRINKING FACT: WORLD

## HOW TO SAY "CHEERS" AROUND THE WORLD

Wales: *iechyd da!*

Japan: *kanpai!*

England: *cheers!*

Italy: *salute!*

Hawaii: *å'kålè ma'luna!*

Germany: *prost!*

China: *ganbei!*

Sweden: *skål!*

France: *à votre santé!*

Greece: *yamas!*

# AUSTRALIA
## CARD
## BLOWING

**Difficulty:**

## What you will need:

Two or more players
A pint of beer
A deck of cards

## Don't blow your chances!

Place a pack of cards on top of a pint glass full of beer. Place the beer in the centre of the table and gather all players around it. Take it in turns to blow the cards off the top of the deck. Sounds easy, but there's a catch! If you blow all or all but one of the cards off the glass, you have to down the pint. A helpful hint: blow from the top of the deck, downward. That way you'll be in less danger of blowing the whole deck off.

# AUSTRALIA
# THE GOON OF FORTUNE

### Difficulty:

### What you will need:

Three or more players
A rotating washing line
A box of wine

## To spin or not to spin.

This is the Aussie staple of drinking games! "Goon" refers to cheap wine, the kind that is housed in a plastic bag within a cardboard box. Start by attaching the bag to a rotary clothes line, or to anything that spins – your imagination may be required here. Once tied, the clothes line is spun. Depending on who the goon bag ends up nearest to, a forfeit or a drinking rule is played. If the bag doesn't land on anyone, the player who has spun the line has to spin themselves round twice and drink some goon. Get the gist?

Great! Now be more adventurous with the rules. The player spins the line, the bag points towards the garden bench; you should turn to the person next to you, pull their socks off with your teeth and take a drink of goon. It points towards a hedge; you should hop on one leg until your next turn.

Continue the game until all players are lying on the floor in a heap of laughter.

# 24 HOURS IN A DAY, 24 BEERS IN A CASE. COINCIDENCE?

**Steven Wright**

# AUSTRALIA
# CHICKEN
# GOGGLES

## Difficulty:

## What you will need:

Three or more players

## We didn't know they needed goggles.

Be warned: do not suggest this party game if your love interest or crush is present – this could get embarrassing! With your fingertips, make goggle shapes and place them over your eyes. Real goggles/glasses are welcome too. It helps if you all sit around a table or in a circle. The starting player shouts, "CHICKEN GOGGLES", followed by a squawk. This continues around to the right.

If a player squawks twice the direction changes to the left.

If a player squawks three times it skips a person.

The first player to make a mistake or hesitate has to down their drink.

# DRINKING FACT: WORLD

## NATIONAL LIQUORS AROUND THE WORLD:

Australia: beer

Belgium: beer

Brazil: cachaça

Cambodia: sombai

China: Moutai

Canada: Canadian rye whisky

Iceland: Brennivín

Egypt: bouza

Germany: schnapps

Greece: ouzo

Ireland: Irish whisky

Japan: shochu

Mexico: tequila

Lebanon: arak

Poland: vodka

Peru: pisco

Trinidad and Tobago: rum

United States: bourbon

# CANADA
# FACEBOOZE

### Difficulty:

### What you will need:

Two or more players
A Facebook account
A smartphone, tablet or computer

# How many "likes" did you get?

Each player must post a Facebook status. It can be anything, but the funnier the status, the quicker the likes will roll in... or so you would hope. Everyone has to drink until they receive a like. Penalties are given to those who write a status beginning with, "Like if you..."

# CANADA
# MOOSE

**Difficulty:**

## What you will need:

Two or more players
Ice-cube tray
Coins
A large glass

## A rather a-moosing game.

First fill the large glass a little way with a drink of your choice and place it by the empty ice-cube tray in the centre of the table. One row of the ice-cube tray should be marked "give one" and the other with "take one".

Players stand around the table and take turns to throw a coin into the tray (it's up to you how many coins you play with). If it lands in the "give one" side, the player must put some of their drink into the large glass at the end of the tray. If the coin lands in the "take one", they must drink from the large glass. If you miss altogether then you down your own drink.

When the last coin is thrown into the tray, all players must raise their arms over their heads like antlers and call out, "MOOSE!" The last player to do this must down the remaining contents of the large glass.

**BEAUTY LIES IN THE HANDS OF THE BEER HOLDER.**

Anonymous

# CANADA
# SHOT
# ROULETTE

## Difficulty:

## What you will need:

Three or more players
An array of alcohol
Shot glasses
An empty bottle

# Spin the Bottle for grown-ups.

Place a bottle in the middle of the table so that it is on its side. This will be used to spin. Arrange the shot glasses in a circle around the bottle and fill with a range of different drinks. Each player takes it in turns to spin the bottle and drink whatever the bottle chooses!

# I'D RATHER HAVE A BOTTLE IN FRONT OF ME THAN A FRONTAL LOBOTOMY.

**Dorothy Parker**

# CHINA
# JIULING

**Difficulty:**

**What you will need:**

Three or more players

# Easy-peasy finger guessing!

This game is a simple one. A chosen player will begin with their hands underneath the table, holding up a number of fingers from one to ten but so no one can see. The other players have to guess how many fingers they are holding up. The person with the closest guess wins that round, while the others drink. Make it harder to guess the number by changing how much a finger is worth – for example, each finger is worth three or six, or thumbs are worth double. Traditionally the losers drink Baiju, a grain-based spirit, but anything with a kick will do!

## DRINKING FACT: CHINA

In China, alcohol is referred to as the "Water of History". This is because tales of liquor can be traced back to almost every period in Chinese history.

# CHINA
# SEVEN

**Difficulty:**

**What you will need:**

Two or more players

## Seven's bad luck.

You play Seven by sitting down in a circle. Go around the circle, counting, but skip over number seven – so six goes to eight – because seven is considered unlucky. As the game goes on it gets harder. Multiples of seven have to be avoided too – 14, 21, 28 and so on. Every time someone gets it wrong, they take a drink and the game begins again at one.

**HEALTH – WHAT MY FRIENDS ARE ALWAYS DRINKING TO BEFORE THEY FALL DOWN.**

**Phyllis Diller**

# CUBA
## CUBAN JENGA

**Difficulty:**

**What you will need:**

Two or more players
A set of Jenga
A marker pen

# Are you Havana good time?

This game involves Jenga blocks, on which you write penalties or even dares before starting — for example, finish your drink, write a 500-word status on Facebook, suck an ice cube for 1 minute. It is just like your usual family game of Jenga but every time the tower is knocked over, the guilty person must take a drink. Every time a penalty or dare is pulled out of the tower the player must do it or they have to finish their drink. Channel your inner Cuban and play this with shots of rum, or at the very least a mojito.

## DRINKING FACT: CUBA

**Ernest Hemingway's favourite drink was the famous Cuban cocktail the mojito. Mojitos were known to cure scurvy in sailors; citrus was one of the best preventatives.**

# ENGLAND

# THE HORSE RACE

**Difficulty:**

**What you will need:**

Two to four players
A deck of playing cards

## Saddle up, drinkers!

Begin by removing all the aces from the deck of cards; these will be your "race horses". Put these to one side for now. Then make a "race track" by placing five to ten cards face down, end to end in a horizontal line. The longer the racing track, the longer the game. Then take your respective "horses" and place them face up in a line perpendicular to the track to create an L shape. All players must then place their bets on the race horse they think will win – for example, I place a bet of two fingers' worth of my drink on diamonds.

You can bet however many fingers' worth you see fit! Make sure someone is jotting down all of the bets; things can get heated in the gambling world.

When all bets have been placed the dealer takes the remaining cards in the pack and turns over the top card. Whichever ace that card corresponds to is moved forward one place. The game is continued until the first ace reaches the end of the track.

The losers drink their bets and the winner chooses a victim for theirs.

# ENGLAND
# THE BOAT RACE

**Difficulty:**

**What you will need:**

An even number of players: six or more

## The English are fond of a jolly good race.

Be warned, this game is fast-paced and can get very messy indeed. Divide yourselves into two equal teams and line each team up so that team members are standing one behind the other. Each of you must have a pint glass full of something lethal in hand. On the count of three the first player in line of each team must begin to drink the entire contents of their pint glass as quickly as possible. When it is empty they must place the pint glass on top of their head.

As soon as this happens the next player must repeat this procedure, as quickly as they can. If a player spills any of their drink or turns their glass over before they are finished, their cup is refilled and they must start again. The same goes for any player who decides to drink prematurely.

The winning team is the first to have all its players finish their drinks. They may then choose a forfeit or drinking penalty for the losing team.

# MAN, BEING REASONABLE, MUST GET DRUNK;

# THE BEST OF LIFE IS BUT INTOXICATION.

**Lord Byron**

# ENGLAND
# TRUE OR FALSE
# STORYTIME

## Difficulty:

## What you will need:

Four or more players
A piece of paper
A dice
A cup
A bowl
A pen

## This one time, I met a jellyfish...

Each player is handed a scrap of paper and has to write one random noun on it. Players fold their piece up and put it into a bowl in the middle of the table.

One at a time, roll the dice in the cup, not letting the other players see what number you have rolled. Then pick a piece of paper from the bowl.

If the dice lands on an even number, you must tell the truth. If the dice lands on an odd number, you must tell a lie. So say the noun on the piece of paper is "jellyfish" and the dice lands on a two, you must tell a truthful story about yourself that involves a jellyfish. However, if the dice landed on a three, you would have to fabricate a story about you and a jellyfish.

Players then have to guess whether the story is true or false. If they are right, you drink; if they are wrong, they drink!

# FRANCE
# BISCUIT

## Difficulty:

## What you will need:

Three or more players
Two dice

## Oh crumbs!

Your first step is to find out which player will be the biscuit. The first person to roll a 7 on the two dice (4+3, 5+2 or 6+1) becomes the biscuit.

The biscuit is then the first to roll the dice. The amount drunk is determined by the numbers the dice fall on. The dice are then passed round the table clockwise.

So the rules are as follows, depending on the numbers rolled on the dice:

1-1: Everyone drinks.

6-6: The roller has to come up with the craziest rule they can think of, and anyone who breaks it must drink.

2-2/3-3/4-4/5-5 (doubles): Roller gives out drinks. For example, 2-2: Roller hands out two drinks.

1-2 (total of 3): Roller has to challenge another player. Both players roll the dice. The player with the highest result wins. The loser has to drink.

3-4, 5-2, 6-1 (total of 7): All players have to put their thumbs on their foreheads and shout, "BISCUITS". The last player to do this downs their drink and becomes the new biscuit.

3-6, 4-5 (total of 9): Person to the right of the roller drinks.

4-6 (total of 10): Roller drinks.

5-6 (total of 11): Person to the left of the roller drinks.

The number 3: If 3 appears, the biscuit has to take a drink. If it's a double 3, the biscuit has to take two drinks, and if 3 is rolled by the biscuit their status is removed and another biscuit is chosen.

## DRINKING FACT:
## FRANCE

**The French are said to consume, on average, 60 litres of wine per person per year.**

# FRANCE
## TOUR DE FRANCE

### Difficulty:

### What you will need:

Two or more players
Shots of vodka
The Tour de France on TV

## On your marks, get set, drink!

Here's what you need to do:

- **When a cyclist breaks away, take a shot of vodka.**

- **When the commentator says a really dull fact – for example, the date a landmark was built – take a drink.**

- **Every time a cyclist throws their water bottle away, drink a shot of vodka.**

- **When a fan runs alongside a cyclist you must drink until they stop running.**

- **When a cyclist falls off their bicycle, down your drink.**

- **When there is a sprint you must drink until the sprint ends.**

If the Tour de France wasn't exciting enough already, this game is sure to make it even better.

And there you have it, your very own Tour de France!

# GERMANY
# FLUNKYBALL

**Difficulty:**

**What you will need:**

An empty beer bottle
Four or more players
A ball

# Bottoms up!

Divide yourselves into two teams and stand facing opposite each other. Everyone needs an alcoholic drink. Place the empty beer bottle between the teams, giving yourselves enough distance from the bottle to make the game challenging. One player from one of the teams throws the ball at the bottle, trying to knock it over. If the player misses, a player from the opposing team throws the ball. If they knock the middle bottle over, their team begins to drink as fast as they can, until the other team stands the bottle upright again and finds the ball, at which point the drinking stops.

The winning team is the team that finishes its drinks first. Good luck!

# GERMANY
## *KASTENLAUF*

### Difficulty:

**What you will need:**

Six or more players
Two crates of beer
A route

## Beer run!

The Germans love to drink and love to run, so this combines both! Hence *Kastenlauf*, or "beer-crate running".

To play you need to split into two teams and map out a running route. Each team has a crate of beer. The course can be anywhere you like, but the Germans typically play around a field or large open area. The length of the race is up to you.

The aim is to cross the finish line, with an empty crate of beers. It is up to each team to decide on a tactic before the run begins. Teams can down the crate at the beginning of the race, down it just before crossing the finishing line or drink as they run.

# Europe's largest consumers of beer per capita are:

1. Czech Republic

2. Austria

3. Germany

4. Estonia

5. Poland

# ICELAND

# *EUROVISION:*
# THE
# DRINKING
# GAME

## Difficulty:

## What you will need:

Five or more players
*Eurovision Song Contest* on TV

# Save your shots for me.

Icelanders love *Eurovision*, so in true spirit, here is a lethal drinking game to go with the competition of the year.

Pick a selection of countries in the final, write them down on pieces of paper, fold the pieces and put them into a bowl or hat.

Each player draws out a country from the bowl/hat: this will be their country for the duration of the game. During the show, players will drink when:

- They see their country's flag

- There is a dramatic key change – Icelanders call it a *Eurovisionhaekkun*

- There is a cliché about peace and love

- A contestant sings with their fists clenched

- A wind machine is used

- There is an on-stage outfit change

- A cheesy stunt is used – for example, a hamster wheel or an ice-skating violinist

- A player's country gets eight points or more

- Or, if you simply feel the need to forget the night, feel free to drink

## DRINKING FACT: ICELAND

In 1915, Iceland banned all alcoholic drinks. Though the restrictions were soon lifted on wine and spirits, beer remained illegal until 1 March 1989, as it was seen as "unpatriotic".

# IRELAND
# IRISH COASTERS

**Difficulty:**

**What you will need:**

Two or more players
Drinks coasters

## Get ready, get set... and flip yer coasters!

This game is played on the bar or on the edge of a table. The simple aim of the game is to flip your coaster and catch it again before it lands. However, as the game progresses this proves a little more difficult than you might expect. Place your coaster on the edge of a flat surface and hit it with your palm. As it is hurled into the air, your task is to catch it again with the same hand you flipped it with. Any player who fails to do this has to drink the entire contents of their full glass.

# IRELAND
## IRISH QUARTERS

**Difficulty:**

## What you will need:

At least four players
One glass per player
A coin

## Spend a penny.

A precursory note: to succeed in this game, drink fast to avoid even more drinking! Each player should fill the cup in front of them with beer. Players take it in turns to spin the coin (or "quarter") on the table. In the time it takes to finish spinning, the player whose go it is has to down their drink and refill their glass ready for their next go. If they fail to do this they can choose either to do a dare or forfeit, decided by the other players, or to down another glass.

So there really is no escape!

I HAVE TAKEN
MORE OUT OF
ALCOHOL THAN
ALCOHOL HAS
TAKEN OUT OF ME.

**Winston Churchill**

# ITALY
## MORRA

**Difficulty:**

**What you will need:**

Two or more players

## Simplicity is next to drunkenness.

This game's a simple one – it seems as though the Italians are just up for a good party! All players sit in a circle or around a table. After a count of three everyone puts one hand in the middle, showing anything from nought to five fingers. Simultaneously all players shout out a guess at the total number of fingers. Whoever guesses the number or gets closest to it wins the round, while all the other players drink.

# JAPAN

# PING PONG PANG

**Difficulty:**

**What you will need:**

Four or more players

*"Iki, iki, iki."*

Japanese drinking games are notoriously difficult, and will usually end in a really crazy night. The more players involved, the more confusing this game will get. One player will start by saying "PING". The person to their left will then say, "PONG", and the next player follows with "PANG" and then has to point to another person to start the cycle again. Players are expected to be drinking throughout the entire game. When a player forgets to say the right word or forgets to point to another player they have to down their drink. Each time a drinking penalty is taken, all players chant *"IKI, IKI, IKI"* until the drink is finished.

# DRINKING FACT: JAPAN

**The Japanese word
for hair of the dog
is *mukai-zake*.**

# JAPAN
# THE
# *ŌSAMA*
# GAME

## Difficulty:

## What you will need:

Three or more players
Same number of chopsticks as there are players

## The King knows best.

*Ōsama* means "king" in Japanese. In this game one player is the King, or *Ōsama*, and the others are numbers. The *Ōsama* must come up with inventive forfeits for his subjects.

To determine the parts that each person will play, write on the thicker end of one chopstick "*Ōsama*" and number the rest. One player must hold all the sticks, covering the end with the numbers on. Each player must pick a stick. The player lucky enough to get the *Ōsama* role must dictate a task and choose the numbers who will do it. At this point in the game it is unknown whose number is whose. For example, "Number 2 must kiss number 5" or "Number 3 must do a silly dance". If players fail to do what the *Ōsama* says, they have to down their drinks, as does anyone else involved in the task. Every time a round of tasks has been completed, chopsticks are gathered up and redistributed again.

# MEXICO
# DUDO

## Difficulty:

## What you will need:

Two or more players
Dice – however many you choose:
the more dice, the more challenging
A cup

# Liar, liar, pants on fire!

This game is usually played with five dice, but you may want to use fewer. Take it in turns to be the roller. The roller puts the dice in a cup and shakes it, then takes a look inside and announces how many have landed on the same number. It is up to the roller to decide if they lie or not – the higher the number of same-number dice, the more fingers each penalty drink is worth. The rest of the players then each state whether they think the roller has lied or not. If one of them says that the roller has lied and the roller is found to have been telling a fib, then the roller has to drink (in this case, it would be five fingers' worth). However, if the roller was telling the truth, then the player to call them a liar takes a drink (again, of five fingers).

# MEXICO
## TOMA TODO

## Difficulty:

## What you will need:

The Mexicans play this with a dreidel
(a small six-sided spinning top),
but a dice will do
Large glass

## Give it all you've got.

The sides of the dreidel are labelled with: *pon uno* (give one), *pon dos* (give two), *pon todo* (give all), *toma uno* (take one), *toma dos* (take two) and *toma todo* (take all). However, you can also use these rules and play with a six-sided dice. Based upon what you roll, either add to the communal glass or drink from it. Play with any drink of your choice, be it beer or something a little stronger to really spice things up!

# DRINKING FACTS: ALCOHOL

Tequila must be produced in Mexico for it to be legitimate.

The Bloody Mary is traditionally a hangover cure; it is consumed in the morning.

According to the Kölsch convention of 1986, it is forbidden to brew Kölsch anywhere other than Cologne, Germany, and it must be consumed at about 10°C in a tall glass, known as a "stange".

Prescribed for numerous medical conditions including period pains, vermouth was made in 400 BCE by Hippocrates, who infused wormwood and dittany flowers in Greek wine.

# MEXICO
# MEXICALI

**Difficulty:**

**What you will need:**

Dice

Three or more players

# It's all about the roll of the dice!

The aim of the game is to get the highest score each round.

Players take it in turns rolling the dice. Before you start, decide how many rolls of the dice you are allowed per person. Rules are as follows:

- **2+1: The highest score you can get.**

- **3+1: The lowest score you can get. In fact, it doesn't count as a throw at all and you must consume all your drink before a new round starts.**

- **Any other combination: you must join the highest score with the lowest, e.g. 1+5=51. The idea is to score higher than your opponents, so if you roll a 2 and a 2, which is a relatively low score, you can roll one dice again – for as many tries as you agreed at the beginning of the game – to try to land the dice on a 1. When you roll again, you are permitted to roll just one dice, if you wish, or you can roll both if neither dice show satisfactory numbers.**

The person who gets the lowest score must drink before the next round begins.

# NORWAY
# COMMANDO
# BIMBALOH

**Difficulty:**

**What you will need:**

Three or more players

## Attention!

One person is chosen as the commander; they will call out commands. The commands are as follows:

- **"COMMANDO BIMBALOH"** is the command for everyone to drum their fingers on the table, as if mimicking a drum roll.

- **"COMMANDO KANT"** is the command for everyone to do a karate chop with both hands.

- **"COMMANDO STOH"** is the command for everyone to place their fingertips on the table, arching their palms like crabs. Both hands should be used.

- **"COMMANDO DOUBLE STOH"** is the command for everyone to place their crab hands one on top of the other.

- **If the commander calls out "BIMBALOH", "KANT", "STOH" or "DOUBLE STOH" without the preceding "COMMANDO" you mustn't perform any command.**

If any player makes a mistake they should drink!

# NORWAY SUBMARINE

**Difficulty:**

**What you will need:**

Four or more players

## Sonar drinking.

All players sit in a circle. As submarines are underwater, players must do the following: holding both hands stretched out in front of your face, make the A-OK sign. Everyone makes a "SHHHH" sound as the submarine descends into water. Each player brings their A-OK signs to their eyes to mean that they are underwater. Now the game may begin.

Submarines use sonar to detect obstacles in the water. This game involves saying "BOOP" to copy the sounds of sonar. If someone says "BOOP" the game carries on clockwise around the circle, until someone says, "BOOP-BOOP". This means that it skips a person. If someone chooses to mimic the sound of the submarine turning around, "WHO- HOO-HOO", then the direction of play changes.

Anyone found to be making a mistake must take a drink.

# RUSSIA
# THE
# TIGER IS
# COMING

## Difficulty:

## What you will need:

Three or more players
Vodka

## Hide!

In true Russian style, the drink you'll need for this game is vodka. One player (usually the lightweight of the group) is chosen to be the game leader, and only drinks every other round. At their discretion they say, "THE TIGER IS COMING!" On hearing this, players have to get underneath the table and take a shot. Players are only allowed to come out from underneath the table when the game leader announces that the tiger has left. The winner is the last person standing (or capable of crouching under the table). The Russians really do know how to drink!

# RUSSIA
## RUSSIAN ROULETTE

**Difficulty:**

**What you will need:**

Two or more players
Six glasses
A dice

# Dare if you will...

Label your glasses from one to six. Fill four of the glasses with water. Then fill two of the glasses with vodka (or white rum or any other clear spirit). If you don't fancy a clear spirit then do it with coloured cups instead. Have the other players turn their backs while shuffling the positions of the glasses. Then repeat the same with another player while you turn your back, so that no one can tell what order the glasses are in. Take it in turns to roll the dice. Whatever number the dice lands on, drink the corresponding glass. If you're feeling adventurous, you can increase the amount – another risky game from the Russians.

**DRINKING FACT: VODKA**

In Slavic languages, *vodka* translates to "little water".

# RUSSIA
# BEAR PAW

**Difficulty:**

**What you will need:**

Three or more players
A large glass

# Beware! Play at your own risk...

To play, fill the large glass with your drink of choice. The Russians traditionally use beer (don't fret, the vodka comes later). Stand in a circle and pass the mug around. Each player must take a drink and then replace what they have drunk with the same amount of vodka. When the mug is filled completely with vodka, the game starts again in reverse, replacing the vodka that has been drunk with beer.

Will you reach the end?

# RUSSIA
# MEDUSA

## Difficulty:

## What you will need:

Four or more players
A table
Shot glasses

## I'm looking at you...

Lay out as many shot glasses as you like on a table. Fill them with your tipple of choice; they could even be jelly shots! All the players should sit around the table in a circular shape so that everyone can see one another. Players begin with their heads down on the table. On the count of three, everyone looks up and stares at another player. If the person you are staring at is looking at someone else, then you are safe. However, if they are returning your stare you both have to drink a shot from the table. This game is repeated until all the shots are gone.

# SOUTH AFRICA
# SPRINGBOKKIES

## Difficulty:

🍷 🍷 🍷 🍷 🍷

## What you will need:

Three or more players
Springbokkie shots

# Don't spill a drop!

A springbokkie shot is as follows:

1 part peppermint liqueur
1 part Amarula Cream

Players should take it in turns to down a springbokkie shot. Easy, right? Wrong! Players have to put their hands behind their backs and stomp their feet alternately while snorting. Then they must pick the shot up with their mouth or teeth and knock it back without spilling it!

## DRINKING FACT: SOUTH AFRICA

In South Africa, the Cape Winelands region is on route 62; this is considered to be the longest wine route in the world. South Africa has the oldest wine industry outside Europe.

# SPAIN
# LOS CHUNGUITOS

**Difficulty:**

**What you will need:**

Four or more players
A Spanish-sounding soundtrack

## There's no taking a siesta in this game!

Start by finding a Spanish-sounding soundtrack or, even better, a song by Los Chunguitos (try YouTube). Sit everyone down in a circle and clap to the beat. One person will start by saying, "I AM CHUNGUITOS NUMBER ONE." This continues round the circle until everyone has a number. Chunguitos number one will then say their number and another player's number. The player who was called out will repeat their own number and call out another. As this is happening, the person sitting to the right of the person whose number has been called must start to imitate an instrument on the track. Once somebody forgets to add an instrument sound, they must take a drink.

## DRINKING FACT: SPAIN

There is a beer spa in Granada that offers beer baths in barrels to its customers. It is said that taking a beer bath has lots of health benefits, including easing muscle tension.

# SPAIN
# BATTLESHIP

## Difficulty:

## What you will need:

Two or more players
A bottle top or a shallow plastic cup
A large glass
A dice

## You sank my battleship!

This is a game said to have originated in Spain because of the sinking of the Spanish Armada. Fill a large glass with your chosen poison and float an upside-down bottle top or shallow plastic cup on top of the liquid. Each player takes it in turns to pour a small measure of their own drink into the floating bottle top or plastic cup. The dice determines the amount that they pour in – e.g. roll a three and three small amounts of the drink are poured in. Whoever sinks or flips the bottle top or plastic cup loses and drinks the contents of the large glass.

**DRINK WHAT YOU WANT, DRINK WHAT YOU'RE ABLE.**

**IF YOU'RE DRINKING WITH ME, YOU'LL BE UNDER THE TABLE.**

**Anonymous**

# SWEDEN
# SEVENS

## Difficulty:

## What you will need:

Five to seven players
A pack of cards

## Spiced-up Scrabble.

First take out the four sevens in the pack of cards and arrange them face up, shortest side of the cards touching, so they form a vertical line on the table. Then deal out the remaining cards in the pack so that each player has the same number.

The objective is to create rows of cards in order, either going up the deck or down. So, for example, if a player has a six of hearts in their hand, they would place it next to the seven of hearts to begin a row. As there are now two cards in this row the player who placed the card down can give out two punishments – either a dare or drink – to a player of their choice. Or they can divvy out the punishments to two separate players. The game progresses and the chains get longer. You could be giving out ten punishments to one person! Just be careful who you make enemies with.

# SWEDEN
# PEN IN
# BOTTLE

## Difficulty:

## What you will need:

Three or more players
Glass beer bottles
String
Pens

## This is a quad workout if you don't succeed first time!

First and most important of all, you need to take your beer bottles and down them. (The quicker you drink them the funnier the game will be.) Take the empty bottles and a long piece of string per person. Take one end of the string and tie it tightly around the pen and then take the other end and tie it around your waist so the pen sits in between the backs of your legs. On a count of three, players need to squat until they manage to successfully get the pen into the beer bottle. If there are more than two of you, the loser downs another bottle of beer with the player who hasn't yet had a turn and they start the game again.

# THE NETHERLANDS
## *PIRAMIDESPEL*

### Difficulty:

### What you will need:

Three or more players
A deck of playing cards

# Can you get to the top of the pyramid?

This is a game of deception: your main aim is to make your opponents drink more than you. The game begins by laying out a face-down pyramid of cards on the table, usually six cards at the base, then five above that, then four, and so on. Each player is then dealt three cards. Each player can only look and memorize these cards once before the game has begun. These cards must be kept a secret from everyone else.

Starting at the bottom left of the pyramid, each player turns over a card; if a player claims to have a card of the same face value, they can nominate someone else to drink. The player told to drink can either do so or they can call the nominating player's bluff. If the nominating player was lying, then they must take a drink. If they were not lying, however, the original victim has to drink double.

Each card that is revealed is replaced by a new one from the deck.

# DRINKING FACT:
## THE NETHERLANDS

Gin was invented
in the Netherlands.
Originally called
jenever, it was used for
medicinal purposes.

# WORLDWIDE
# AROUND THE WORLD

## Difficulty:

## What you will need:

Three or more players

 # Maps at the ready!

You can do this with countries, continents and place names, but celebrities from around the world can work too! Player one begins by naming any noun from the chosen category, and the next player must name another that begins with the last letter of the previous word. For example, if player one says Brazil, the next player might say Latvia, followed by Afghanistan, and so on.

Any player to hesitate for more than three seconds or make a mistake has to take a drink!

IF THIS DOG
DO YOU BITE,
SOON AS OUT
OF YOUR BED,
TAKE A HAIR OF
THE TAIL THE
NEXT DAY.

Scottish proverb

# HAPPY DRINKING!
# PLEASE ALWAYS DRINK RESPONSIBLY.

Have you enjoyed this book? If so, find us on Facebook at Summersdale Publishers, on Twitter at @Summersdale and on Instagram at @summersdalebooks and get in touch. We'd love to hear from you!

www.summersdale.com